ECONOMIC CARTOONS

 Glencoe

New York, New York   Columbus, Ohio   Chicago, Illinois   Woodland Hills, California

TO THE TEACHER

Economic Cartoons *provide high-interest visualization of concepts that you want to teach. These cartoons challenge students to apply what they have learned in the text. Using cartoons also allows students with weaker reading skills to develop higher level critical thinking skills such as:*

- Understanding the use of caricature, satire, and irony

- Understanding cause-effect relationships

- Comparing and contrasting

- Writing opinions, creative solutions, and interpretations

You may want to use a cartoon as a beginning class activity, a lesson illustration, a review activity, or follow-up activity. Several cartoons may be chosen for an in-depth lesson on interpreting economic cartoons. Each cartoon activity begins with low level multiple choice questions designed to help students identify the symbols and characters in the cartoon. Critical thinking questions follow, asking students to analyze the cartoon and express their own opinions or to apply what they have learned in creative ways.

CREATING A CUSTOMIZED FILE

*The individual booklets in the **Teacher's Classroom Resources** provide a wide variety of supplemental materials to help make economics meaningful to students. These resources appear as individual booklets in a carryall file box.*

There are a variety of ways to organize Economic Cartoons classroom resources. Three alternatives are given here:

- **Organize by category** (all activities, all tests, etc.)

- **Organize by category and chapter** (all Chapter 1 activities, all Chapter 1 tests, etc.)

- **Organize sequentially by lesson** (activities, quizzes, and other materials for Chapter 1, Section 1; Chapter 2, Section 2, etc.)

Regardless of the organization you choose, you may pull out individual activity sheets from these booklets, or you may photocopy them directly from the booklets and file the photocopies. You will then be able to keep original booklets intact in a safe place.

Glencoe

Send all inquiries to:

Glencoe/McGraw-Hill

8787 Orion Place

Columbus, OH 43240

ISBN : 978-0-07-878055-4

MHID : 0-07-878055-1

Printed in the United States of America

1 2 3 4 5 6 7 8 9 10 047 10 09 08 07

CONTENTS

ECONOMIC CARTOON I

CHOICES, CHOICES

Economics is first, and finally, about choices. What to make? What to buy? How much to spend? The way individuals and businesses choose to answer such questions is the stuff of economics. It is also the stuff of political cartoons, since many economic choices are controversial.

Directions: *Study the cartoon below. Then answer the questions that follow.*

c1998Wiley Miller, The Washington Post Writers Group. Reprinted with permission.

EXAMINING THE CARTOON

◉ Multiple Choice

1. What economic choice or choices are symbolized by the cartoon?

    a. the economic choice to hire cheaper labor   **b.** the economic choice to reduce business costs

    c. the economic choice to enhance a company's image   **d.** all of the above

2. Whom do the men with briefcases symbolize?

    a. a particular business   **b.** a particular industry   **c.** any business   **d.** large firms

3. Which word best describes the cartoonist's view of the choices that big business tends to make?

    a. self-serving   **b.** altruistic   **c.** careful   **d.** rash

◉ Critical Thinking

4. Analyzing the Cartoon How do Santa Claus and the businessmen create a strong contrast?

_____

_____

5. Expressing Your Opinion Do you think the Santa's workshop idea is effectively used in this cartoon? Why or why not?

_____

_____

_____

ECONOMIC CARTOON 2

Ⓦ HO GETS THE CREDIT? WHO TAKES THE BLAME?

The American economy is a unique mix of business activity and government action. The government, simultaneously, tries to help control the economy and to let markets function freely. This "mixed" economic system has proved effective, but the economy isn't always humming. When there are problems, both the public and private spheres look for someone to blame.

Directions: *Study the cartoon below. Then answer the questions that follow.*

AFFIXING BLAME FOR OUR ECONOMIC PROBLEMS

Paul Conrad, Los Angles Times Syndicate.

ECONOMIC CARTOON 2

EXAMINING THE CARTOON

◉ Multiple Choice

1. Who are the people pictured in the cartoon?

   a. fictional business people   **b.** former U.S. presidents   **c.** symbolic consumers   **d.** ordinary citizens

2. What distinguishes the figures in the foreground from those above and behind?

   a. The figures in the foreground are business people.
   b. The figures in the foreground were alive when the cartoon was published in 1981.
   c. The figures in the foreground are government officials.
   d. The figures in the foreground are wealthy.

3. Look at the figure in the upper left. Which is the best interpretation of the significance of where he is pointing?

   a. It establishes that the figure in the lower left is ultimately to blame.
   b. It establishes that none of the figures is willing to accept blame.
   c. It establishes that he is the first figure in the series.
   d. It has no significance in the overall message of the cartoon.

◉ Critical Thinking

4. **Analyzing the Cartoon** Write a one-sentence summary of the message of this cartoon. Then explain how you could update this cartoon.

   _____

   _____

5. **Expressing Your Opinion** Do you think the cartoonist effectively gets his message across? Explain.

   _____

   _____

   _____

☞ **P9-AQL-330**

ECONOMIC CARTOON 3

PRODUCER PAINS

Ergonomics is the science concerned with human engineering—arranging things in the environment so that people and the things they use interact most efficiently. For example, efficiency in production might be increased by changing the height of a worker's chair.

Directions: *Study the cartoon below. Then answer the questions that follow.*

Steve Kelley

EXAMINING THE CARTOON

◉ Multiple Choice

1. The stars and stripes identify the character riding on business's shoulders as

   a. a consumer.   **b.** foreign competition.   **c.** U.S. government.   **d.** private industry.

2. The cartoonist believes government is often

   a. supportive of business.   **b.** a hindrance to business.   **c.** an enemy of business.   **d.** unaware of business.

◉ Critical Thinking

3. **Analyzing the Cartoon** What is the irony illustrated by the two statements in the cartoon?

   _____

4. **Expressing Your Opinion** Write a short paragraph agreeing or disagreeing with the point of view of the cartoonist.

   _____

Economic Cartoons

ECONOMIC CARTOON 4

① DEMAND!

Demand is a fundamental concept in economics. It is perhaps best defined as what people in the marketplace want to buy and at what price. But demand can get complicated. To truly understand demand, one needs also to understand the law of demand, quantity demanded, the demand curve, the elasticity of demand, and many other concepts. An imperfect understanding of demand can lead to some interesting results, as you shall see.

Directions: *Study the cartoon below. Then answer the questions that follow.*

CALVIN AND HOBBESc Watterson. Reprinted with permission of UNIVERSAL PRESS SYNDICATE. All rights reserved.

ECONOMIC CARTOON 4

EXAMINING THE CARTOON

⦿ Multiple Choice

1. The boy in the cartoon is named Calvin. What role does Calvin claim to play in his lemonade business?

    a. owner   **b.** president and CEO   **c.** employee   **d.** all of the above

2. Which group of people does the cartoon indict?

    a. workers   **b.** stockholders   **c.** business people   **d.** all of the above

3. What is ironic about the statement "Caveat emptor [let the buyer beware] is the motto we stand behind!"?

    a. *Caveat emptor* is a motto of consumer caution—not something for a business to "stand behind."

    b. *Caveat emptor* is a motto for huge, multinational firms—not a lemonade stand.

    c. *Caveat emptor* is a nonsense term—something a small child would make up.

    d. *Caveat emptor* is a Latin phrase—it has nothing to do with business.

⦿ Critical Thinking

4. Analyzing the Cartoon Identify at least five different political statements this single cartoon makes.

_____

_____

5. Expressing Your Opinion Which political statements identified in your answer to question 4 do you agree with? Explain why you think each one is fair or not.

_____

_____

_____

ECONOMIC CARTOON 5

SANTA: A SLOPPY SUPPLIER?

The supply of goods and services in the American economy is fundamentally affected by competition. What products are supplied, how they are supplied, who supplies them, where and when they are supplied—all are largely determined by competition among suppliers. When the level of competition changes, the effects on consumers can be dramatic.

Directions: *Study the cartoon below. Then answer the questions that follow.*

Calvin and Hobbes   by Bill Watterson

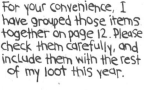

CALVIN AND HOBBESc Watterson. Reprinted with permission of UNIVERSAL PRESS SYNDICATE. All rights reserved.

EXAMINING THE CARTOON

⦿ Multiple Choice

1. This cartoon can be read and enjoyed on several levels. Which statement best captures the economic message of the cartoon?

   a. "Materialism increases the quantity demanded."   **b.** "Consumer demand is elastic."

   c. "Monopolies negatively affect consumers."   **d.** "Supply is related to demand."

2. What is *economically* wrong about the interpretation the boy makes in the last panel?

   a. Santa Claus doesn't really exist.   **b.** Santa Claus does have competition.

   c. Santa Claus is not a manufacturer.   **d.** Santa Claus does not charge for goods.

3. Assume the assessment of Santa Claus the boy makes in the last panel is correct. How would competition make him less "sloppy"?

   a. Competition forces suppliers to improve service.   **b.** Competition has a direct effect on the quantity supplied.

   c. Competition increases the elasticity of supply.   **d.** Competition creates supply.

⦿ Critical Thinking

4. **Analyzing the Cartoon** What can you infer about the boy from the third panel of the cartoon?

   _____

   _____

5. **Expressing Your Opinion** Identify and explain what you think is the central message of the cartoon.

   _____

ECONOMIC CARTOON 6

 ## VALUE OR STATUS? WHY PEOPLE BUY WHAT THEY DO

The U.S. economy has a circular flow: income flows continuously between businesses and consumers. Income flows from businesses to consumers in the form of wages, interest, and profits. Income flows from consumers to businesses in the form of payments for consumer services and goods. What consumers choose to buy, therefore, is a fundamental part of the economy. Such buying decisions are influenced by many factors: price, quality—and status. One observer of the American economy has identified the role of status in a cartoon about ramen noodles—an inexpensive Asian food that comes in small, meal-sized packages.

Directions: *Study the cartoon below. Then answer the questions that follow.*

Scott Bateman

ECONOMIC CARTOON 6

EXAMINING THE CARTOON

◉ Multiple Choice

1. Who got more ramen noodles for his money?

    a. the man on the left   **b.** the man on the right

    c. they both got the same deal   **d.** it is impossible to tell

2. Why is the man on the left panel excited?

    a. He has discovered a new food.   **b.** He has increased his income.

    c. He has benefited from a sale.   **d.** He has outdone the other man.

3. How would you characterize the other man's response?

    a. friendly   **b.** frustrated   **c.** excited   **d.** snobbish

◉ Critical Thinking

4. Analyzing the Cartoon Why would the second man feel superior for paying *more* for the product? Explain.

_____

_____

5. Expressing Your Opinion Do you think snobbery or value plays a bigger role in most consumer buying decisions? Explain your answer.

_____

_____

_____

ECONOMIC CARTOON 7

LET THE BUYER BEWARE

The Latin phrase caveat emptor *means "let the buyer beware" or "buy at your own risk." Consumers are wise to keep it as their motto. After all, those who market goods are working in their self-interest to sell them. The relationship between selfish business interests and victimized consumers is a favorite topic of cartoonists.*

Directions: Study the cartoon below. Then answer the questions that follow.

THE FAR SIDE   By GARY LARSON

EXAMINING THE CARTOON

◉ Multiple Choice

1. What does the "rolls a little rough" statement about a rock that is obviously flat on the bottom imply about this salesperson's attitude toward consumers?

   a. They really need this product.   **b.** They are very gullible.
   c. They need encouragement to make the decision.   **d.** They can't afford anything better.

2. What message does the "prehistoric" setting of the cartoon convey?

   a. Consumers have always been victimized.   **b.** Transportation has always been a need.
   c. People have always bought and sold things.   **d.** Civilization has made great advances.

◉ Critical Thinking

3. **Analyzing the Cartoon** How do the hanging flags enhance the point of the cartoon?

   _____

4. **Expressing Your Opinion** Do you think this cartoon qualifies as an editorial, or is it only intended to make people laugh? Explain.

   _____

ECONOMIC CARTOON 8

A REAL GAME OF MONOPOLY?

Microsoft Corporation is a computer industry giant. Its operating systems run more than 90 percent of the personal computers in the world. When Microsoft integrated its newest operating system with its own Internet software, other software firms cried foul. They claimed that Microsoft was seeking to use its control of operating system software to gain control of the market for application programs. Was Microsoft becoming a monopoly? In an antitrust lawsuit brought by the Justice Department, a court ruled that it was. The judge ordered the breakup of Microsoft. This ruling was later overturned on appeal, and the Justice Department announced that it would no longer seek to break up Microsoft. The case was settled with what critics saw as merely a slap on the wrist of the corporate giant.

Directions: Study the cartoon below. Then answer the questions that follow.

OLKIPHANTcUNIVERSAL PRESS SYNDICATE. Reprinted with permission. All rights reserved.

ECONOMIC CARTOON 8

EXAMINING THE CARTOON

● Multiple Choice

1. What does the cartoon imply about the outcome of the Justice Department's lawsuit against Microsoft?

    a. Microsoft would lose.   **b.** The Justice Department would win eventually.

    c. The Justice Department would have difficulty winning. **d.** Microsoft would win on appeal.

2. A reasonable interpretation of the cartoon would be that the government

    a. should not try to interfere in the economy.   **b.** has difficulty controlling such a powerful company.

    c. is not competent enough to regulate the economy.   **d.** is supportive of big business.

● Critical Thinking

3. Analyzing the Cartoon Create an appropriate title or caption for the cartoon.

_____

4. Expressing Your Opinion Do you think the cartoon is effective in making its point without text? Explain.

_____

_____

_____

_____

ECONOMIC CARTOON 9

CONSUMER: A TOUGH ROLE

The role of the consumer is a tough one to play. The scenery consists mostly of advertisements, the other actors are often fast-talking salespeople, and the audience confers status on the basis of what one buys. Cartoonists have become some of the most effective critics of this materialistic play-acting.

Directions: *Study the cartoon below. Then answer the questions that follow.*

Jim Borgman, *Cincinnati Enquirer*, June 10, 1990.

Jim Borgman / Reprinted with special permission of King Features Syndicate.

ECONOMIC CARTOON 9

EXAMINING THE CARTOON

⦿ Multiple Choice

1. What is the cartoonist indicting?

   a. the lack of support for recycling   **b.** a materialistic culture

   c. excessive advertising   **d.** any or all of the above

2. The figure in the cartoon represents which of the following?

   a. consumers   **b.** advertisers   **c.** marketers   **d.** business owners

3. What market failure is illustrated by this cartoon?

   a. the creation of large amounts of waste   **b.** inadequate public transportation

   c. the creation of an underclass   **d.** insufficient social services

⦿ Critical Thinking

4. **Analyzing the Cartoon** The figure in the cartoon is free to recycle; no one would prevent him. Why, then, is he sighing?

   _____

   _____

5. **Expressing Your Opinion** Explain why you agree or disagree with how the cartoonist has depicted the consumer culture in the United States.

   _____

   _____

   _____

ECONOMIC CARTOON 10

 A **NATION ON CREDIT**

At the close of the twentieth century, credit card use in the United States reached an all-time high. Millions of people, whose parents and grandparents believed in "living within your means" and "paying as you go," made a different economic choice: to "buy now and pay (with interest) later." These people were often enticed by credit card companies, who made it easy to get a credit card with a high credit limit (the amount of money one can charge to a card).

Directions: Study the cartoon below. Then answer the questions that follow.

JEFF STAHLER reprinted by permission of Newspaper Enterprise Association, Inc.

EXAMINING THE CARTOON

◉ Multiple Choice

1. What is the most shocking information in the woman's statement?

    a. that the mail is on time   **b.** that there is so little mail

    c. that the credit limits are so high   **d.** that there are only two bills

2. Why did the cartoonist not put an exclamation point after the ridiculously high credit limits?

    a. to convey the idea that high credit limits are becoming customary

    b. to show that the woman does not understand credit

    c. to raise doubts about this couple's credit

    d. to support the idea of high credit limits

◉ Critical Thinking

3. **Analyzing the Cartoon** How does the cartoonist use exaggeration to make the point?

_____

ECONOMIC CARTOON 11

BUYING A HOME

For many Americans, owning their own home is more than meeting a basic need; it is the fulfillment of the American dream. One common sticking point in the home buying process is escrow (also referred to as closing or settlement): the depositing of a sum of money with a third party (the escrow agent) who sees that the transfer of funds from the seller to the buyer takes place once all the terms of the contract have been agreed upon and fulfilled. Coming up with escrow money, agreeing on the terms of its release, and completing the mountains of paperwork involved has frustrated thousands of home buyers.

Directions: *Study the cartoon below. Then answer the questions that follow.*

c1992 Wiley Miller, The Washington Post Writers Group. Reprinted with permission.

EXAMINING THE CARTOON

◉ **Multiple Choice**

1. Who does the person under the boulder represent?

    a. an escrow agent   **b.** a home buyer   **c.** a real estate agent   **d.** a home seller

2. What message does the "prehistoric" setting of the cartoon help convey?

    a. that there has always been a housing shortage   **b.** that buying a home today is much more complicated

    c. that shelter has always been a necessity of life   **d.** that civilization has made great advances

3. What do you think is the purpose of this cartoon?

    a. to make a complex policy argument   **b.** to change escrow laws

    c. to make people laugh   **d.** to criticize a political party

◉ **Critical Thinking**

4. **Analyzing the Cartoon** Do you think the cartoonist had a particular audience in mind for this cartoon? Explain.

    _____

5. **Expressing Your Opinion** Evaluate this cartoon. Do you think it makes an important point? Is it amusing? Is it effective? Explain why you think it does or does not qualify as a good economic cartoon.

    _____

ECONOMIC CARTOON 12

IT'S A WILD RIDE

The Dow Jones Averages are indexes that investors use to judge the overall performance of the stock market. Each index tracks the prices of several of the most widely held U.S. stocks.

Directions: *Study the cartoon below. Then answer the questions that follow.*

"Dow Jonesy enough for you?"

Jack Ziegler/www.cartoonbank.com

EXAMINING THE CARTOON

⊙ Multiple Choice

1. The cartoonist is comparing the stock market to

   a. an amusement park.
   c. a roller coaster.
   b. the Dow-Jones Industrial Average.
   d. a winding road.

2. According to the cartoon, the stock market is about to

   a. go down.
   c. go up.
   b. stabilize.
   d. crash.

⊙ Critical Thinking

3. **Analyzing the Cartoon** What is the nature of the stock market, according to the cartoonist?

   _____

   _____

4. **Expressing Your Opinion** Given its nature, would you invest in the stock market? Why or why not?

   _____

   _____

ECONOMIC CARTOON 13

QUESTION OF ECONOMIC EQUALITY

Achieving equal wages has been a long-term battle for women. Today, on average, women doing the same job as men still make less money. Moreover, a disproportionate number of high-level jobs still go to men. This situation makes an easy target for a savvy editorial cartoonist.

Directions: *Study the cartoon below. Then answer the questions that follow.*

Doug Marlette

EXAMINING THE CARTOON

◉ Multiple Choice

1. What American tradition is the basis for the cartoon?

    a. striving to achieve a white-collar job
    b. framing the first dollar one ever earns
    c. taking pride in one's work
    d. doing the best job one can

2. What is the relationship between the jobs of the two people?

    a. They are in equivalent jobs.
    b. The woman has a higher level job than the man.
    c. The man has a higher level job than the woman.
    d. There is no relationship between their jobs.

3. Which economic concept is illustrated by the cartoon?

    a. equilibrium
    b. comparable worth
    c. circular flow of income
    d. comparative advantage

◉ Critical Thinking

4. **Analyzing the Cartoon** What two points about the job market is the cartoonist making?

    _____

    _____

5. **Expressing Your Opinion** Do you think this cartoon has the power to change a reader's mind? Explain.

    _____

Economic Cartoons

ECONOMIC CARTOON 14

FLIGHT OF THE IRS

The Internal Revenue Service (IRS), charged with collecting taxes, is quite possibly everyone's least favorite government agency. Under fire in recent years for using bullying tactics, it's no wonder that the IRS is a favorite target of political cartoonists.

Directions: *Study the cartoon below. Then answer the questions that follow.*

"I WONDER DO YOU EVER AUDIT YOURSELVES...? JUST JOKING JUST JOKING."

"REMEMBER—POLITE AND COURTEOUS, MY PRETTIES!"

OLIPHANT©UNIVERSAL PRESS SYNDICATE. Reprinted with permission. All rights reserved.

EXAMINING THE CARTOON

◉ Multiple Choice

1. What movie does the cartoon allude to?

    a. *Gone With the Wind*   **b.** *The Wizard of Oz*   **c.** *Casablanca*   **d.** *The Phantom Menace*

2. Where are the flying monkeys going?

    a. to collect taxes   **b.** to report to Congress

    c. to audit taxpayers   **d.** to pay for government programs

◉ Critical Thinking

3. Analyzing the Cartoon What is the significance of the witch's words to the monkeys?

_____

4. Expressing Your Opinion Do you think the commentary by the small characters in the lower left adds to or detracts from the cartoon? Why?

_____

ECONOMIC CARTOON 15

THE SHIRT OFF LINCOLN'S BACK

In the late 1980s the federal government began to spend what would eventually total about 200 billion dollars of taxpayer money to bail the savings and loan industry out of a financial crisis of its own making. The move was widely viewed as benefiting the rich at the expense of the lower and middle classes.

Directions: *Study the cartoon below. Then answer the questions that follow.*

"Looks like the S & L rip off is worse than we thought."

Steve Benson

EXAMINING THE CARTOON

◉ Multiple Choice

1. What is the setting of this cartoon?
   - **a.** Washington Monument
   - **b.** White House
   - **c.** Capitol
   - **d.** Lincoln Memorial

2. What is the cartoonist's attitude toward the bailout of the savings and loan industry?
   - **a.** He is supportive.
   - **b.** He opposes it.
   - **c.** He is ambivalent.
   - **d.** He views it as a necessary evil.

◉ Critical Thinking

3. **Analyzing the Cartoon** What about the setting of this cartoon makes it especially effective?

_____

4. **Expressing Your Opinion** Do you think the federal government should help businesses overcome their financial mistakes? Explain.

ECONOMIC CARTOON 16

THE PENALTY FOR EARLY WITHDRAWAL

Banks offer higher interest rates on certificates of deposit (CDs) than on passbook savings accounts. If you invest in a CD, you agree to leave the money on deposit for a specified period of time. If you take the money out early, the bank will charge a substantial penalty.

Directions: Study the cartoon below. Then answer the questions that follow.

"Who knew there'd be such a substantial penalty for early withdrawal."

Patrick Hardin/www.cartoonresource.com

EXAMINING THE CARTOON

◉ Multiple Choice

1. In the cartoon, what is the penalty for early withdrawal?

    a. large fee   **b.** execution

    c. counseling   **d.** jail

2. What technique does the cartoonist use to create humor?

    a. caricature   **b.** exaggeration

    c. pun (double meaning)   **d.** sarcasm

◉ Critical Thinking

4. Analyzing the Cartoon What details does the cartoonist use to suggest where the people are?

_____

5. Expressing Your Opinion Do you think it is fair for banks to charge a penalty for early withdrawal from a CD? Why or why not?

_____

ECONOMIC CARTOON 17

DAY TRADING—BIG WINNINGS, BIG LOSSES

Using high-speed Internet connections, day traders, for a fee, can buy and sell stocks on a moment's notice. A sophisticated trader can make a great deal of money by taking advantage of small variations in stock prices. The danger is that most day traders are not so sophisticated and lose a great deal of money.

Directions: *Study the cartoon below. Then answer the questions that follow.*

Jeff MacNelly

EXAMINING THE CARTOON

◉ Multiple Choice

1. What becomes of the man shining shoes in the first panel?

   a. He turns to day trading.   **b.** He becomes wealthy.

   c. He loses his money in the stock market crash.   **d.** It is impossible to tell.

2. What does the cartoon imply will happen to the man in the second panel?

   a. He will become a professional broker.   **b.** He will lose his money.

   c. He will invest in Internet stocks.   **d.** It is impossible to tell.

◉ Critical Thinking

3. **Analyzing the Cartoon** What is significant about "1929"?

   _____

   _____

4. **Expressing Your Opinion** Do you think day trading should be legal? Explain.

   _____

Economic Cartoons

ECONOMIC CARTOON 18

WHAT ECONOMIC INDICATORS REALLY INDICATE

"Leading economic indicators" are the best tools we have to evaluate the current state of the economy and to predict what is likely to happen in the future. The way economic indicators are calculated is often a subject of debate, however, since so much can ride on measurements such as the Consumer Price Index (CPI).

Directions: Study the cartoon below. Then answer the questions that follow.

John Trevor, Albuquerque Journal c1996

EXAMINING THE CARTOON

◉ Multiple Choice

1. What is the CPI supposed to reflect?

    a. the cost of living   **b.** unemployment   **c.** American exports   **d.** the national debt

2. Why does the man in the cartoon decide not to challenge the CPI?

    a. because he agrees it is properly calculated   **b.** because adjusting it would cost him

    c. because it is a government figure   **d.** because the official and actual CPIs coincide

◉ Critical Thinking

3. **Analyzing the Cartoon** Whom do you think the man in the cartoon is supposed to represent? Explain.

_____

4. **Expressing Your Opinion** Do you think the attitude of the man in the cartoon reflects the attitude of most Americans? Why or why not?

_____

_____

ECONOMIC CARTOON 19

WOULD YOU LIKE FRIES WITH THAT?

The late twentieth century was marked by many paradoxes in the American economy. One was the layoff of tens of thousands of white-collar workers in the midst of an economic boom. Many were middle-aged and were forced, late in life, to change jobs and even careers to find work in what was called "the new economy."

Directions: *Study the cartoon below. Then answer the questions that follow.*

Mike Keefe

EXAMINING THE CARTOON

◉ **Multiple Choice**

1. What is the speaker training the audience to do?

    a. regain their jobs   **b.** improve their attitudes

    c. work in a fast-food restaurant   **d.** collect unemployment

2. What is the attitude of the speaker?

    a. glib   **b.** frustrated   **c.** helpful   **d.** indifferent

◉ **Critical Thinking**

3. **Analyzing the Cartoon** What is ironic about the "service" that the corporation seems to be offering to its employees?

_____

4. **Expressing Your Opinion** Do you think that corporations have a responsibility to find jobs for the people they lay off? Explain your position.

_____

ECONOMIC CARTOON 20 💰

THE POWER OF THE FED

The Federal Reserve Board's decision to raise or lower interest rates can have a profound effect on business activity. Comments by the chairman of the Fed often signal the Fed's intentions. So when the chairman speaks, investors respond. At the time this cartoon was published, the chairman of the Fed was Alan Greenspan.

Directions: *Study the cartoon below. Then answer the questions that follow.*

c1997 Jimmy Margulies, The Record, New Jersey reprinted by permission.

EXAMINING THE CARTOON

⊙ Multiple Choice

1. What do the stocks listed on the board have in common?

   a. They are all medicines.   **b.** They are all treatments for symptoms of anxiety.

   c. They are all increasing in value.   **d.** all of the above

2. What can you infer about "Greenspan's comments"?

   a. They were positive observations about the economy.   **b.** They encouraged investment in drug companies.

   c. They were considered bad news by investors.   **d.** They discouraged investors from panicking.

⊙ Critical Thinking

3. **Analyzing the Cartoon** Do you think the cartoonist is approving, disapproving, or neutral toward the Fed chairman's influence? Explain.

   _____

4. **Expressing Your Opinion** How firmly based in reality do you think this cartoon is? Explain your opinion.

ECONOMIC CARTOON 21

THE END OF AN ERA

Generations of Americans grew up going to "Woolworth's." The venerable five-and-dime store originated in 1879 and became a presence in virtually every downtown in the United States. But changes in consumer preferences forced Woolworth Corporation to do away with its namesake general merchandise stores. Shoppers turned away from the homey stores—which often featured a lunch counter—to huge discount stores and specialty retailers.

Directions: *Study the cartoon below. Then answer the questions that follow.*

c1997 Jimmy Margulies, The Record, New Jersey reprinted by permission.

EXAMINING THE CARTOON

◉ **Multiple Choice**

1. What is the basic message of the cartoon?

   a. Wal-Mart has taken over Woolworth's business. **b.** Discount chains are winning in the marketplace.

   c. Americans no longer value the five-and-dime. **d.** all of the above

2. Which economic concept or concepts are illustrated by the cartoon?

   a. supply and demand **b.** risk and competition

   c. capitalism and economic choices **d.** all of the above

◉ **Critical Thinking**

3. **Analyzing the Cartoon** Imagine that the cartoon includes a person looking in through the store window. Write an appropriate comment for that character to make.

   _____

4. **Expressing Your Opinion** Do you think America has benefited or suffered from the growth of huge discount chains like Wal-Mart? Explain.

   _____

ECONOMIC CARTOON 22 💰

ⒼUESS WHO'S COMING TO DINNER

China's 1.3 billion people represent a huge potential market for U.S. businesses. As president, Bill Clinton (shown as a boy in the cartoon) tried to improve trade relations with China. His efforts were controversial. China's Communist government still controlled much of the economy, and it was accused of human rights abuses.

Directions: *Study the cartoon below. Then answer the questions that follow.*

Lurie's NewsCartoon

"Guess who's coming to dinner?"

Lurie / Cartoonews International Syndicate

EXAMINING THE CARTOON

⦿ Multiple Choice

1. What does the man in the chair represent?

   a. parents   **b.** the United States   **c.** the world   **d.** Congress

2. Why is China portrayed as a giant?

   a. because it is a Communist country   **b.** because it has a history of human rights abuses

   c. because it is very populous   **d.** because it has a powerful military

⦿ Critical Thinking

3. **Analyzing the Cartoon** What is the significance of the fact that China is "stained"? What does this say about the cartoonist's view of China?

_____

4. **Expressing Your Opinion** Do you think the United States should maintain trade relations with a country that has a bad human rights record? Explain.

_____

ECONOMIC CARTOON 23 💰

A PYRAMID SCHEME

About three out of every four people in the world today live in developing countries. Located mostly in Africa, Asia, and Latin America, these countries have tried many programs to improve their economies, with varying degrees of success.

Directions: *Study the cartoon below. Then answer the questions that follow.*

"WHEN WE BUILT IT WE THOUGHT IT WOULD SPUR ECONOMIC DEVELOPMENT IN THE AREA...."

Jim Borgman / Reprinted with special permission of King Features Syndicate

EXAMINING THE CARTOON

◉ Multiple Choice

1. What has the artist chosen the pyramid to represent?
   - **a.** corrupt rulers
   - **b.** elaborate attempts at economic improvement
   - **c.** all ancient monuments
   - **d.** complex and well-planned building projects

2. Who is the cartoon criticizing?
   - **a.** Arabs
   - **b.** tourists
   - **c.** Egyptians
   - **d.** developers

◉ Critical Thinking

3. **Analyzing the Cartoon** Imagine a similar cartoon that pictured another famous monument in its setting—like the Eiffel Tower or Taj Mahal. How would this change the point of the cartoon?

_____

4. **Expressing Your Opinion** Do you think tourist attractions can help developing nations? Why or why not?

_____

ECONOMIC CARTOON 24 💰

THE GLOBAL ECONOMY: HANGING TOGETHER

The late twentieth-century was marked by economic globalization. International trade reached record levels and people spoke in glowing terms about "the global economy." However, another aspect of globalization is interconnectedness. If one country experiences economic difficulty, it may be felt across international borders. This cartoon reflects the positives and potential negatives of the global economy.

Directions: *Study the cartoon below. Then answer the questions that follow.*

Steve Lindstrom

EXAMINING THE CARTOON

⦿ Multiple Choice

1. What does the cartoon imply about the Asian economy?

   a. that it is dependent on the European economy   **b.** that it is crashing

   c. that it is prospering   **d.** that it is stagnant

2. What does the rope symbolize?

   a. economic ties, like trading   **b.** political ties, like treaties

   c. social ties, like travel   **d.** geographic ties, like shared borders

3. What view of the global economy does the cartoonist express?

   a. that Americans are opposed to it   **b.** that it can be dangerous

   c. that most countries benefit from it   **d.** all of the above

⦿ Critical Thinking

4. **Analyzing the Cartoon** What is the significance of the fact that each walking figure is both holding the rope and has it around his neck?

   _____

5. **Expressing Your Opinion** Do you agree with the cartoonist's opinion of the global economy? Explain.

   _____

Cartoon 1

Multiple Choice

1. d

2. d

3. a

Critical Thinking

4. Answers will vary, but students should note the contrast between the altruism of Santa Claus and the selfishness of the businessmen.

5. Answers will vary, but students should support their opinions. Most students will probably feel that the idea of a business having to use elf labor shows how serious the corporations believe the issue of cheap overseas labor to be. It also gives the cartoon an imaginary and ironic tone that helps to make the point.

Cartoon 2

Multiple Choice

1. b

2. b

3. a

Critical Thinking

4. The cartoon establishes that presidents tend to blame the previous administration for any current economic problems. The cartoon could be updated by adding pictures of the presidents after Reagan, each pointing to the previous one, and by having Washington point at the current president.

5. Answers will vary, but students should support their opinions.

Cartoon 3

Multiple Choice

1. c

2. b

Critical Thinking

3. The businessman is complaining about a pain in the neck caused by a government that is announcing plans to alleviate such pains through ergonomic standards.

4. Answers will vary, but students should support their opinions.

Cartoon 4

Multiple Choice

1. d

2. d

3. a

Critical Thinking

4. The cartoon criticizes businesses for overcharging; stockholders, executives, and employees for greed; businesses for rationalizing low-quality products and for irresponsibility toward the environment; conservatives for attacking any criticism of business; and the hypocrisy of business interests in seeking subsidies.

5. Answers will vary, but students should support their opinions.

Cartoon 5

Multiple Choice

1. c

2. d

3. a

Critical Thinking

4. Answers will vary, but students should note that the boy, who alludes to "page 12" and "loot," is materialistic.

5. Answers will vary, but students should support their opinions. The message seems to be the materialism of the boy, or of children in general these days.

Cartoon 6

Multiple Choice

1. a

2. c

3. d

Critical Thinking

4. Answers will vary, but students should allude to the ironic snobbishness of consumers who take pride in paying more for an equivalent good, status-seeking, materialism, and the like.

5. Answers will vary, but students should support their opinions. Snobbery or status can certainly be a force in buying decisions.

Cartoon 7

Multiple Choice

1. b

2. a

Critical Thinking

3. Answers will vary, but students should note the prevalence of such flags at modern car dealerships.

4. Answers will vary, but students should support their opinions. The cartoon is humorous, but it was created as a commentary on the subject, and not just to entertain.

Cartoon 8

Multiple Choice

1. c

2. b

Critical Thinking

3. Answers will vary, but students should demonstrate an awareness of the message of the cartoon. Sample answer: "The Big-Game Hunters"

4. Answers will vary, but students should justify their opinions.

Cartoon 9

Multiple Choice

1. d

2. a

3. a

Critical Thinking

4. Answers will vary, but students should note that in such a materialistic culture where there is so much pressure to consume, recycling is a never-ending process.

5. Answers will vary, but students should support their opinions.

Cartoon 10

Multiple Choice

1. c

2. a

Critical Thinking

3. The "$3.2 million" credit limit is an exaggeration that highlights how credit card companies tempt consumers.

Cartoon 11

Multiple Choice

1. d

2. b

3. b

Critical Thinking

4. Answers will vary, but students might suggest that the cartoon would appeal to anyone who has felt frustration over the complexity of the home-buying process.

5. Answers will vary, but students should justify their opinions.

Cartoon 12

Multiple Choice

1. c

2. a

Critical Thinking

3. Answers will vary, but students should note that the stock market goes up and down, and it can be a wild ride.

4. Answers will vary, but students should support their opinions. Even though the stock market has its ups and downs, wise investing is still the best way to make your money grow.

Cartoon 13

Multiple Choice

1. b

2. c

3. b

Critical Thinking

4. Answers will vary, but students should express an understanding that women are often underpaid compared with men and do not have equal access to high-level jobs.

5. Answers will vary, but students should support their opinions. Political cartoons can influence public opinion.

Cartoon 14

Multiple Choice

1. b

2. c

Critical Thinking

3. After criticism of IRS tactics, the IRS promised to reform their practices.

4. Answers will vary, but students should support their opinions. The commentary underscores the basic point of the cartoon.

Cartoon 15

Multiple Choice

1. d

2. b

Critical Thinking

3. Answers will vary, but students should allude to Lincoln as an honest "man of the people" and to the Lincoln Memorial as a "sacred" public place; both facts stand in contrast to the firms that benefited from the savings and loan industry bailout.

4. Answers will vary. Some students may feel that it is the government's responsibility to help save major businesses if it affects jobs, investors, or the national economy. Others may feel that businesses must suffer for their own mistakes and not be saved with taxpayers' money.

Cartoon 16

Multiple Choice

1. d

2. b

Critical Thinking

3. Students should note the striped clothing, bars on the window, and stark furnishings.

4. Answers will vary, but students should support their opinions. Students should recognize that depositors receive a higher interest rate on CDs in exchange for agreeing to leave the money in the CD for a certain time period. They pay a penalty fee for breaking this agreement.

Cartoon 17

Multiple Choice

1. c

2. b

Critical Thinking

3. Answers will vary, but students should show that they understand that (amateur) investor optimism was misplaced in the time just before the 1929 stock market crash, and that day traders today are likely to suffer the same fate.

4. Answers will vary, but students should support their opinions. Many people have called for the abolition of day trading, while others view it as an individual's right.

Cartoon 18

Multiple Choice

1. a
2. b

Critical Thinking

3. Answers will vary, but students should explain their answers. The man is a symbol of people who criticize politics but hypocritically want it to serve their own interests.

4. Answers will vary, but students should support their opinions.

Cartoon 19

Multiple Choice

1. c
2. a

Critical Thinking

3. Answers will vary, but students should demonstrate that they understand that the corporation is helping employees find new jobs, but that the new jobs are not of the quality of the old ones, so it is not really help at all.

4. Answers will vary. Some students may feel that it is the responsibility of the company to help workers find new jobs; others may feel that the company does not owe former employees any assistance.

Cartoon 20

Multiple Choice

1. d
2. c

Critical Thinking

3. Answers will vary, but students should explain their interpretations. The cartoonist is at least taking note of the Fed chairman's influence.

4. Answers will vary, but students should support their opinions. The reflection of the Fed chairman's influence is realistic, especially his ability to affect the stress levels of investors; his effect on particular drug stocks is highly doubtful.

Cartoon 21

Multiple Choice

1. d
2. d

Critical Thinking

3. Answers will vary, but students should demonstrate an understanding of the basic message of the cartoon. Sample answer: "I never thought I'd see the day."

4. Answers will vary. Some students may argue that large chains offer lower prices and one-stop shopping. Others may feel that stores like Wal-Mart kill competition, erode community centers, and negatively affect the landscape.

Cartoon 22

Multiple Choice

1. b
2. c

Critical Thinking

3. Answers will vary, but students might indicate that the cartoonist views closer ties to China as a dangerous policy given the stains on China's record.

4. Answers will vary. Some students may feel that the US should maintain trade relations with China because it is a large market and a powerful country. Others may feel that the US should not maintain trade with a country with a poor human rights record and which has stolen military secrets.

Cartoon 23

Multiple Choice

1. b
2. d

Critical Thinking

3. Answers will vary, but students should demonstrate an understanding of the basic point of the cartoon: that current economic development projects are being juxtaposed with a huge ancient building project.

4. Answers will vary. Some students may feel that tourist attractions may help an area by bringing in people who will spend money; others may feel that spending money on elaborate and expensive projects when people don't have adequate necessities of life is wasteful.

Cartoon 24

Multiple Choice

1. b
2. a
3. b

Critical Thinking

4. Answers will vary, but students might note that holding the rope represents voluntary participation in the global economy, while the position of the rope around each figure's neck represents the possibility of hanging, or suffering from the voluntary participation.

5. Answers will vary, but students should support their opinions.